AF487927

Adventurous
Cheerful
Open-minded
Forgiving
Special
Persistent
Loving
Vivacious
Intentional
Mindful
Inventive
Humble
Heroic
Wise
Determined
Compassionate

IT'S OKAY!

Written By: Michelle Daniels-Holloway

Illustrated By: Mehk Arshad

This book is dedicated to my precious baby cousin Kasandra, who passed away during the process of my writing this book. She lived a life that fully embraced it being 'OKAY' to just be you! I love you so much, baby girl… Fly high!

BE KIND

It's OKAY to be loving,
accept others and be kind.
Even if they are "different,"
from what you have in mind.

SCIENCE

BE DIFFERENT

It's OKAY to be weird or different,
there is only one YOU.
You were made to accomplish things,
only you can DO.

BE CURIOUS

It's OKAY to be curious,
life can be a mystery.
Your journey in this life
can help you rewrite history.

BE BRAVE

It's OKAY to be ambitious.
It's OKAY to be brave.
Your inner voice will always guide you,
your heart knows the way.

BIG

DREAM BIG

It's OKAY to believe,
you were created to dream!
You can imagine BIG ideas,
no one else has ever seen!

Love,
Peace & Unity

BE THE CHANGE

It's OKAY to speak out loud!
Your gift is your voice.
You can lead others and change lives,
you've been given that choice!

It's OKAY to be quiet,
and preserve your energy.
We gain wisdom when we listen,
and learn from what we see.

BE STRONG

It's OKAY to do your best.
It's OKAY to be strong.
It's OKAY to make mistakes.
It's OKAY to be wrong.

It's OKAY to have morals,
in life, they'll take you far.
Like a compass, they will guide you,
and be your north star

AUDITIONS

It's OKAY not to be okay.
Life is not always kind.
You carry the power to move mountains,
it all starts in your mind.

BE PATIENT

It's OKAY to be patient,
patience has its own pace.
Just relax and let it flow,
it will all be worth the wait.

It's OKAY to just BE YOU.
It's OKAY to run your race.
You were made for a great purpose,
you are loved in countless ways.

About the Author

A Texas native, Michelle Daniels-Holloway is a mommy, educator, author, public speaker, entrepreneur, podcaster, and the founder/CEO of the Los Angeles County-based youth organization, S.P.E.A.K. OUT LOUD. Michelle has over 20 years of experience and is passionate about positively impacting youth, along with teaching all ages to discover their identity and become the very best version of themselves.

Smart
Helpful
Peaceful
Loved
Brave
Creative
Amazing
Courageous
Intuitive
Unique
Brilliant
Funny
Be Yourself
Strong
Beautiful
Polite
Kind
Intelligent
Ambitious
Generous
Curious